MERRILL READING PROGRAM

DIG IN

FIFTH EDITION

Cover Foreground, ©Patrick Morrow/Adventure Photo & Film; Cover Background, © K. Chiang/Superstock

Based on the philosophy of Charles C. Fries

Authors

Phyllis Bertin
Educational Coordinator
Windward School
White Plains, New York

Dr. Cecil D. Mercer
Professor of Education
University of Florida
Gainesville, Florida

Eileen Perlman
Learning Disabilities Specialist
White Plains Public Schools
White Plains, New York

Mildred K. Rudolph
Rosemary G. Wilson

Columbus, Ohio

A Division of The McGraw·Hill Companies

TABLE OF CONTENTS

On Jan's Lap	6
Nat and Rags	7
Can It Fit?	8
Sam and Rags	9
Nat and the Map	10
Tin Cans	12
Dan's Fan	13
A Pin for Jan	14
A Fat Pin	15
Jam for Dan and Jan	16
I Am Tam	18
Tags and Bags	19
A Cap in a Bag	20
Fix With Pins	21
Jan's Maps	22
Lids for Pans	24
A Tin Lid	25
Sid and the Van	26
Jan's Cap	27
Sid and the Tin Lid	28
Jim, Kim, and Jan	30
For Dan	31
For Jan	32
A Bad Rim	33
A Tin Can and a Tin Lid	34
Zip the Bag	36

SRA/McGraw-Hill
A Division of The McGraw-Hill Companies

Copyright © 1999 by SRA/McGraw-Hill. All rights reserved. Except as permitted under the United States Copyright Act, no part of this publication may be reproduced or distributed in any form or by any means, or stored in a database or retrieval system, without prior written permission from the publisher.

Printed in the United States of America.

Send all inquiries to:
SRA/McGraw-Hill
8787 Orion Place
Columbus, Ohio 43240-4027

ISBN 0-02-674707-3

6 7 8 9 BCH 06 05 04

Sid's Lip	37
A Rip in a Bag	38
Figs and a Wig	40
Dig for Dad	41
In the Pit	42
Not in the Sun	44
Six Buns	45
Pins for Caps	46
Not a Bit for Rags	47
Bat a Run	48
A Big Bun	50
A Big Pig	51
A Cut in a Bag	52
Not for Rags	53
Fix a Fan	54
A Cut Lip	56
Tam's Pup	57
The Pup and the Cup	58
A Bug in the Van	60
A Bug on a Rug	61
A Bad Pup	62
Fun for Jim and Kim	64
On the Bus	65
Six on a Bus	66
Kim and Little Bud	68
Little Pam	69
Mud on the Van	70
Gum for Pam	72
Not Fit for a Pup	73
Mud on a Pup	74
A Pup and a Cub	76
Suds on a Pup	77
To the Teacher	78

bit bits
fit fits
hit hits
sit sits

it's

fat   sat   bat   at
fit   sit   bit   it

On Jan's Lap

Can Nat sit on Jan's lap?

Nat can sit on her lap.

Nat sat on Jan's lap.

Rags ran to see Jan.

Can she and Nat fit on Jan's lap?

She and Nat can fit.

Jan pats Rags and Nat on her lap.

Nat and Rags

Nat sits on Sam's lap.
Sam pats the cat.

Rags can see Nat on Sam's lap.
She is sad.
Can Rags fit on Sam's lap?
She can.

Rags and Nat nap.

Can It Fit?

Sam had a hat in a bag.
It's not his hat.

Is it for Dan?
Sam fits the hat on Dan.
It fits!
It is Dan's hat.

Sam and Rags

Sam and Rags sat in the van.
Sam had a ham in a bag.
It's a fat ham.
Rags bit the bag.

Is Sam mad at Rags?
He is not mad.
Sam had ham bits for Rags.

She wags and wags.

Nat and the Map

Sam had a map in the van.
Nat looks at it.
Nat hits and hits the map.
He hit it and bit it.

Sam had to look at the map.
It's in bits!
He looks at Nat.

Bad Nat!
It's bad to hit Sam's map!

pin   pins
win   wins
tin

into

pan	pin	tin	win
pin	tin	win	pin
			tin

Tin Cans

Jan sees a tin can.
She fits it into her bag.

Dan sees a tin can.
He fits it into his bag.

Jan and Dan ran for cans.
Cans in bags win pins.

Dan's Fan

Dan had a fan.
Rags can see it.
She bit the fan.

Dan ran to Rags.
Rags!
Not the fan!

The fan is tin!
It can hit Rags.
Rags is sad.

A Pin for Jan

A man had pins for caps.
The man sees Dad.
Can Dad win a pin for Jan's cap?

Dad wins a pin.
He pins it on her cap.
Jan had a pin on her cap.

A Fat Pin

Look at Jan's cap.
A fat pin is on it.

Jan taps the tin pin.
The pin is on her lap.

Jan is not mad.
She can fit the pin on her cap.

Jam for Dan and Jan

Dad had jam for Dan and Jan.
It's in a tin can.
Rags sees the jam.
She sits and looks into the can.

Dan and Jan look at Rags.
The jam is not for Rags.
It's for Jan and Dan.

Rags is sad.

six

fix

mix

sat	fat	six	fix
sit	fit	mix	six
six	fix		mix

I Am Tam

I am Tam.
I am in the van with Dan
and Jan.
Sam had to fix the van.

I can look at his maps.
Jan and Dan can tag and bat.
Sam can fix the van.

Tags and Bags

Tam is in the van.
"I can mix the tags on the bags,"
she said.

Sam looks for his bag.
He took a bag.
The bag is not his.

Sam looks at Tam.
"It's bad to mix tags on bags,"
he said.

Tam is not sad.
She can fix the tags.

A Cap in a Bag

Dan's cap is on a mat.
Nat looks at the cap.
He bit it and hit it.
He hit it into a bag.

Dan had to look for his cap.
Tam is with Dan.
"Look in the bag, Dan," she said.

Dan said, "It's in the bag.
It's a rag!"

Fix With Pins

Tam's cap is in bits.
"I can fix it with pins," said Dan.

He pins the bits into the cap.
"It's a bad fit," said Tam.

"I can fix it," Dan said.
With six pins, he pins the cap.
It fits!

Jan's Maps

Jan looks for her maps.
"I had six maps in the van,"
she said.

"Tam took the six maps," said Dad.

Jan ran to Tam.
"I had six maps in Dad's van,"
said Jan.

Tam had the maps with her.
She took the maps to Jan.
Jan took the six maps to the van.

did

lid   lids

hid

rid

Sid

cannot

(got)   (of)

hat	sat	Dad	lid
hit	sit	did	did
hid	Sid	lid	rid

Lids for Pans

Sam had six pans in his van.
He had lids for the pans.
Tam took a pan with a lid.
Nat took the lid and hid it.

Sam said, "Tam, fix a lid
for the pan."

Tam got tin to fit the pan.
She said, "Nat is bad.
He hid the lid for the pan."

A Tin Lid

A tin lid is on the pan.
The lid did not fit the pan.
Nat hit at it.
Dad cannot nap.

Dad took the lid and hid it.
"I got rid of it," he said to Dan.
"I hid it."

Nat looks for the lid.

Sid and the Van

I am Sid.
I can fix a van.

The van had a bad fan.
The fan hit the van.
I can tap a pin into the fan.

I see bits on the fan.
With a rag, I got rid of the bits.

I did fix the van.

Jan's Cap

Tam hid Jan's tan cap.
She hid it in a bag.
Jan looks and looks for her cap.
She looks into the bag.

"Nat is a bad cat,"
Jan said to Tam.
"He hid the tan cap."

Tam said, "He did not.
I hid it."

Sid and the Tin Lid

Sid ran her van.
The lid for a pan is
in the van.
Sid said, "Is a tin can
in the van?"

She looks into the van.
"It's not a can," she said.
"It's the lid for a pan.
Dan's dad hid it in the van."

Sid got rid of it.

him
rim
Jim
Kim

me

ham	jam	him	Kim
him	Jim	Jim	him
		Kim	rim

Jim, Kim, and Jan

Sid took Jim and Kim to see Jan.

Jim, Kim, and Jan ran.

Jan said, "Look at me!

Can Kim tag me?"

Kim ran at Jan.

Kim tags her.

Jim ran and hid.

Jan and Kim had to look for him.

"Jim hid," said Jan.

"I cannot see him.

He wins!"

For Dan

Sam had a bag in his van.
A tag is on the bag.
It said, "For Dan."
In the bag is a bat for him.

Kim looks into the bag.
"Is the bat for me?" she said.

"It's for Dan," said Sam.
"I hid it in the bag."

For Jan

Dan took his bat to Jan.
"See the bat Sam got for me?"
Dan said to her.
Jan looks at Sam.
Sam had a bag with a tag.

"Is it for me?" Jan said.

The tag said, "For Jan."
In the bag is a bat for Jan.

A Bad Rim

Jim and Kim had Nat's pan.
The pan had a bad rim.
Jim took the pan to his dad.

Kim said, "Nat had a pan
with a bad rim."

Jim said, "It's bad for him.
He cannot lap at his pan."

"The rim is tin," said Dad.
"I cannot fix it."

Jim got rid of the pan.

A Tin Can and a Tin Lid

Dad had ham in a tin can.
A lid fits on the rim of the can.

Jim and Kim look at the can.
"Is the can tin?" said Jim.

"And the lid?" said Kim.
"Is the lid tin?"

"The lid is tin," said Dad.
"And the can is tin."

lip   lips
dip   dips
tip   tips
rip   rips
zip   zips

has

as

lap	tap	tip	rip
lip	tip	lip	dip
		rip	zip

Zip the Bag

Jim cannot zip his bag.
It has a bad rip in it.
He took the bag to Kim.

Kim has pins to fix the bag.
She tips the bag to look
at the rip.
She pins it.

Jim looks at the bag
as Kim zips it.

Sid's Lip

Sid bit her lip.

Tam has a kit.
She can fix Sid's lip.

Sid has to sit for Tam
to fix her lip.
Tam dips the tip of a pad into
a can.
She pats Sid's lip with the pad.
She fits the pad on Sid's lip.

A Rip in a Bag

Jan has ham in a bag.
Dan has to dip into the bag
for a bit of ham.
He rips the bag.

Jan looks at the bag.
She sees the rip in it.
She looks at Dan.
Dan has bits of ham on his lips.

big
fig   figs
wig   wigs
pig   pigs
dig   digs

if

happy

| bag
big | wag
wig | big
wig
pig | pig
fig
dig |

Figs and a Wig

Tam has a tan wig.
Kim has a bag of figs.
Tam took a fig and ran.

"If Tam took a fig,
I am mad," said Kim.
Kim is not a bit happy.
She took Tam's wig.
She hid it in a bag.

"Wigs for figs," said Kim.
Tam took the fig to Kim.
Kim took the wig to Tam.

Dig for Dad

Dad is not happy.
He has to dig a big pit.
He digs and digs.

Dad said, "I had to dig a big pit, and I did."
He sat and took a nap.

Jan said, "Rags and I can dig a big pit."

Jan and Rags dig a pit for Dad.

In the Pit

Nat digs in Dad's pit.
He hid his pan and lid in it.
Rags digs in the pit.
She hid a tin can in it.

Dad looks into his big pit.
He said, "A can, a pan, and a lid?
Did pigs dig in the pit?"

"Rags and Nat did it," said Jan,
"not a pig.
Rags is not a pig.
Nat is not a pig."

run	runs
bun	buns
fun	
sun	

(your)

ran	fan	fun	run
run	fun	run	sun
		sun	bun

Not in the Sun

"Jim, run and tag me.
It's fun," said Tam.

"Not in the sun," said Jim.
"It's not fun if I run
in the sun."

Tam runs to Kim.
"Run and tag me," she said.

"It's not fun to run in the sun,"
said Kim.

"I can run in the sun,"
said Tam.
"It's fun for me!"

Six Buns

Kim ran and got six buns
for her dad.
She took the buns to him.

"I got six big buns,"
she said to him.

"Six buns in a bag," said Dad.

"A bun for me, a bun for Dan,"
said Kim.
"A bun for Jan, a bun for Tam.
And buns for Dad and Jim."

Pins for Caps

Jim had a pin on his cap.
Kim said, "Is the pin
on your cap tin?"

"It's a tin pin," said Jim.

Jan's cap has a pin on it.
"I had to run to win it,"
said Jan.

Jan and Jim had pins.
Kim did not.
Jim said, "If Kim runs,
she can win a pin."
Kim said, "Is it fun to run?"

Not a Bit for Rags

Tam took a bun to Jan.
The bun had bits of fig in it.
Rags looks at the bun
and wags at Tam.

Jan said, "Fix a bit of your bun
for Rags, Tam."

"A bun with figs is bad for Rags,"
said Tam.

Rags is not happy.
She is sad.

Bat a Run

Dan is not happy.
He had to bat in a run to win.
He said, "I cannot bat if I look into the sun."

His dad said, "Fix your cap."

Dan did as his dad said.
He bats in a run and wins.

but

cut   cuts

nut   nuts

hut   huts

(have)

bat	but	but	cut
bit	cut	cut	nut
but		hut	but

A Big Bun

Sid had a big bun in a bag.
The bun had nuts on it.
Sid said, "I have to cut the bun
into six bits."

She rips the bag and cuts the bun.
"I have a bun with nuts,"
said Sid.
"I have bits of bun for Jim, Kim,
Dan, Jan, Tam, and me."

A Big Pig

Dad and Dan sat in the van.
"Look at the huts," said Dad.

A man ran pigs into a hut.
A big pig did not run.
The man had to tap the pig.
The pig got in, but it got mad.

"The big pig cannot have fun in the hut," said Dan.

A Cut in a Bag

Jim has a bag,
but he cannot zip it.
He took it to his dad.
His dad can fix it for him.

Jim's dad has to cut into the bag.
He cuts and cuts.

Kim said, "Look, Jim!
Look at the big cut in your bag!"

Jim's dad said, "It's a big cut,
but I can fix it."
And fix it he did.

Not for Rags

Tam got buns for Jan and Dan.
She got big buns
with nuts and figs.
She had to cut the buns.
Rags looks at a bun
with a nut on it.

Tam cut the buns.
She had a bit for Jan and for Dan,
but not for Rags.
"Rags cannot have nuts," she said.
Rags is sad.

Fix a Fan

Sid has a fan,
but the fan cannot run.
It has a bad rim.

Sid looks for Dan's dad.
"I can fix a van, but I cannot
fix a fan," Sid said to him.

Dad tips the fan and looks at it.
He cuts a bit of tin.
He taps it on the bad rim.

"Your dad can fix fans,"
said Sid to Dan.

cup   cups

pup   pups

up

cap	cup	pup	up
cup	pup	up	cup
			pup

A Cut Lip

Jim cut his lip on a cup.
Tam took Jim and the cup
to her dad.
She said, "Look
at Jim's lip, Dad.
He cut it on a cup."

Dad said, "Look up at me, Jim.
I have to look at your lip.
It's bad to have a cup
if it cuts your lip."

Jim looks up as Tam's dad fits
a pad on his lip.
Tam got rid of the cup.

Tam's Pup

Tam has a tan pup.
Dan said, "Tam, look at your pup.
He has a cup, and it has
a bad rim."

The pup runs to Tam with the cup.
He sits up for Tam,
but she is not happy.

"Pups cannot have cups
with bad rims," she said.
The pup sits on Tam's lap,
and she pats him.

The Pup and the Cup

Tam got rid of the cup
with the bad rim.
But her pup digs it up.
He runs to Rags with it.
Rags and the pup run and run
with the cup.

Kim said to Tam, "Your pup has
the cup with the bad rim.
It can cut him."

Tam ran to Rags and the pup.
She took the cup and hid it.

bug   bugs
jug   jugs
hug   hugs
rug   rugs
tug   tugs

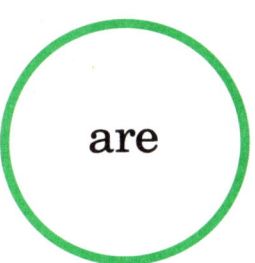

bag	rag	tag	bug
big	rug	tug	hug
bug		hug	jug

A Bug in the Van

Jan is in the van with Kim.
Jan looks up and sees a bug.
She tugs at Kim.
"Look, Kim," she said.
"It's a big bug!"

"It's not a bad bug," said Kim.
She hugs Jan, but Jan
is not happy.

"Hit it," said Jan.
Kim fans at the bug and taps it.
The bug runs.
Kim got rid of the bug.
Jan has a hug for Kim.

A Bug on a Rug

Jim and Kim sit on a rug.
A bug runs on the rug.
It runs into Kim's jug.
It runs into Jim's cup.

"Hit the bug with your cap!"
said Jim.
Kim hits it, and the bug runs.
Jim and Kim are happy
to see the bug run.

A Bad Pup

"Tam's pup is bad," said Jan
to Kim.
"He tugs at rugs.
He bats at bugs.
He tips jugs.
He digs in pits.
He is a bad pup."

"He is not bad," said Kim.
"He is a happy pup,
and happy pups dig and tug."

bus

Gus

us

bag	bus	up	Gus
bug	Gus	us	bus
bus			us

Fun for Jim and Kim

Jim and Kim are with Jan.
Jim said to Jan, "Gus took us
on his bus.
He took us to look at the pigs.
Gus had to fix the bus,
and I sat with him.
I had maps to look at.
Kim ran to look at the pigs."

Jan said, "It's fun to look
at pigs in huts!"

"But I had fun with Gus
and the maps," said Jim.

On the Bus

Gus runs a big bus.
Jan and Tam are on the bus.
Tam has her pup on her lap.
Kim runs to sit with Jan
and Tam.
"I have a bun for us," she said.
She cuts the bun into bits.

"Have a bit of bun," she said
to Tam's pup.
The pup wags and wags.
Kim hugs the pup.

Six on a Bus

Jim and Kim are on a bus.
Jim said, "Look at us
on a big bus.
We are with Gus,
and he runs the bus.
Jan and her dad are with us.
Six of us are on the bus."

Kim said, "It's not six, is it?"

Jan said, "It is six.
Rags got on with us."

mud

Bud

suds

(little)

mad	bad	Sid	Bud
mud	Bud	Sid's	mud
		suds	suds

Kim and Little Bud

Kim and Pam are on the bus with Gus.
Kim sees her cat, Little Bud.
"Gus, look at Little Bud!"
she said.
She ran and got the cat.

But Little Bud is in the mud.
Kim got mud on her and mud on the bus.
She and Gus are not a bit happy.

Little Pam

Gus is Pam's dad.
Little Pam took him to look at
the pigs in the huts.

Pam ran to look at the pigs.
Gus said, "Pam!
Look at your hat!
It's in the mud!"

Gus had to dip into the mud
for Pam's hat.
Pam is sad, but Gus said,
"A little bit of suds
can fix your hat."

Mud on the Van

Pam and Kim are with Sam
in his van.
The van ran into the mud.
Pam said, "Look at the mud
on the van.
I have to have rags
and a pan of suds."

Pam got the pan of suds.
Kim got the rags.
Pam and Kim dip into the suds.

Kim, Pam, and Sam got rid
of the mud on the van.

hum   hums

gum

ham	hum	gum	hum
him	gum	hum	hums
hum			

Gum for Pam

Gus has a little bag for Pam.
Pam sees gum in the bag.
"Kim can have gum," said Pam.
"But I cannot see Kim."

Gus said, "Run to Kim with the gum."
Pam is happy.
She hums as she runs.

"It is fun to have gum," she said.
"It is fun to hum."

Not Fit for a Pup

Pam had a bag with gum in it.
Her pup bit into the bag.
The gum is in the mud.
The pup ran to Kim with the gum.
Kim said to Pam, "Your pup
has gum with mud on it."

Kim tugs at the gum,
but the pup runs to Pam.
Pam took the gum.
She said, "It's not fit for me,
and it's not fit for a pup.
It has mud on it."

Mud on a Pup

Pam's pup ran into the mud.
He ran into the mud for the gum.
"Pam! Your pup has mud on him!"
said Kim.

Pam said, "I have rags
and a pan of suds for us."
Pam hums as she dips the rags
into the suds.
"I got rid of the mud
on the pup," she said.

Her pup wags and wags.

rub   rubs
tub   tubs
cub   cubs

rag	tag	tub	cub
rug	tug	rub	cubs
rub	tub	cub	rubs

A Pup and a Cub

Pam's pup is in the tub,
and Pam rubs him with a rag.
Tam runs in.

"Pam cannot have cubs in tubs,"
she said to Pam.

"It's not a cub," said Pam.
"It's a pup!"

"Can I rub suds on the pup?"
said Tam.

Tam and Pam rub suds on the pup.

Suds on a Pup

Pam's pup runs up to Kim.
He has suds on him.

Kim said, "I have a tub
and a rag.
I can rub Pam's pup."
She rubs and rubs.

Kim took the pup to Pam.
"Wag for Kim," said Pam
to her pup.
"She got rid of the suds."

TO THE TEACHER

The MERRILL READING PROGRAM consists of eight Readers developed on linguistic principles applicable to the teaching of reading. The rationale of the program and detailed teaching procedures are described in the Teacher's Edition of each Reader.

All words introduced in this Reader are listed on the following pages under the headings "Words in Pattern," "Sight Words," and "Applications of Patterning."

Words listed as "Words in Pattern" represent additional matrixes in the first major set of spelling patterns. Pattern words introduced in this Reader have the matrixes *-it, -in, -ix, -id, -im, -ip, -as, -ig, -un, -ut, -up, -ug, -us, -ud, -um,* and *-ub.* The one-word pattern *if* is also presented. The consonant letters *k, z,* and *g* appear in initial positions for the first time. In addition, some pattern pages present combinations of words (compound words) and pattern words with the ending *-s.*

Words listed as "Sight Words" are high-frequency words introduced to provide normal sentence patterns in the stories.

Words listed as "Applications of Patterning" include new words based on patterns and sight words previously introduced, additional tense forms, plurals, and possessives.

WORD LISTS FOR TEACHER REFERENCE

Pages	Words in Pattern	Sight Words	Pages	Words in Pattern	Sight Words
Unit 1 5-10	bit bits fit fits hit hits sit sits it's	for	Unit 7 39-42	big fig figs wig wigs pig pigs dig digs if	happy
Unit 2 11-16	pin pins win wins tin into		Unit 8 43-48	run runs bun buns fun sun	your
Unit 3 17-22	six fix mix	took with said	Unit 9 49-54	but cut cuts nut nuts hut huts	have
			Unit 10 55-58	cup cups pup pups up	
Unit 4 23-28	did lid lids hid rid Sid cannot	got of	Unit 11 59-62	bug bugs jug jugs hug hugs rug rugs tug tugs	are
Unit 5 29-34	him rim Jim Kim	me	Unit 12 63-66	bus Gus us	
			Unit 13 67-70	mud Bud suds	little
Unit 6 35-38	lip lips dip dips tip tips rip rips zip zips has as		Unit 14 71-74	hum hums gum	
			Unit 15 75-77	rub rubs tub tubs cub cubs	

Applications of Patterning
(The underlined numbers are page numbers.)

Unit 1 5-10 looks	Unit 4 23-28 pans tan	Unit 7 39-42 pit	Unit 10 55-58 rims	Unit 13 67-70 Pam Pam's
Unit 2 11-16 cans caps sees	Unit 5 29-34	Unit 8 43-48	Unit 11 59-62 Kim's pits	Unit 14 71-74 . . . .
Unit 3 17-22 tags Tam Tam's	Unit 6 35-38 kit pad Sid's	Unit 9 49-54 fans Jim's	Unit 12 63-66	Unit 15 75-77 . . . .